BULLYPROOF YOURSELF

Virender Kapoor is a thinker, an educationalist and an inspirational guru. An alumnus of IIT Bombay, he also holds a master's degree in International Relations and Strategic Studies from Savitribai Phule Pune University. His books on emotional intelligence and leadership have been translated into several regional and foreign languages. A prolific writer, he regularly contributes to *The Times of India*, *The Economic Times*, *Rediff.com* and several management magazines. To know more about him, log on to www.virenderkapoor.com. He can be reached at virenderkapoor21@yahoo.com.

Also by the author:

Speaking: The Modi Way

Leadership: The Gandhi way

Innovation: The Einstein Way

Excellence: The Amitabh Bachchan Way

Winning: The Chanakya Way

Resilience: The Hawking Way

Succeeding: The Akshay Kumar Way

Mission Accomplished: Applying Military Principles to Real Life

Creative Entrepreneurship: The Walt Disney Way

BULLYPROOF YOURSELF

Empowering You to Become **Resilient**

VIRENDER KAPOOR

RUPA

Published by
Rupa Publications India Pvt. Ltd 2023
7/16, Ansari Road, Daryaganj
New Delhi 110002

Sales centres:
Bengaluru Chennai
Hyderabad Jaipur Kathmandu
Calcutta Mumbai Prayagraj

P-ISBN: 978-93-5702-658-1
E-ISBN: 978-93-5702-784-7

First impression 2023

10 9 8 7 6 5 4 3 2 1

Printed in India

Contents

Preface

While writing schoolbooks on values for students of Class 1 to Class 8, I had to sift through a plethora of topics related to child psychology. At the same time, I interacted with more than a hundred teachers, parents and principals to understand the fundamental problems and how to address them in a comprehensible manner.

This informal survey with parents and teachers provided me with what I call the 'windsock feel': to know clearly which way the wind is blowing. Somehow, I could gauge the pulse of the topic 'bullying' quite well out of this.

I wanted to write a practical guide—a book that would empower children and the youth. Today's world is competitive; there is a shortage of resources and little peace in any part of the globe. We have made progress and got comfort with the rise of technology, but we are rapidly moving away from being humane.

'Perform or perish' and 'hit the ground running' are the more recent corporate and entrepreneurial slogans. People are as if on a treadmill and the incline keeps becoming steeper and steeper. Hence, a book like this one becomes the need of the hour.

Introduction

'Self-defense is not only our right; it is our duty.'

—Ronald Reagan

I had the privilege of writing books, doing talk shows and workshops for school students, graduates and industry professionals on emotional intelligence (EQ), human competence, human behaviour and passion quotient.

There are hundreds of books on bullying and how to prevent it. Most of these books put the onus of preventing bullying on schools and its authorities. Character building, too, is assumed to be only the school's responsibility, though a large portion of the responsibility actually rests with the parents. Rules, standard operating procedures and legislative laws are becoming stricter and stricter as far as bullying is concerned.

While the rules for preventing bullying should

be stringent, do we empower every child to be self-sufficient and face the world? I think we don't.

Parents blindly believe that their child is the best, most obedient and, of course, most brilliant. They fail to understand the fine line between loving and pampering a child. One should not pamper a child so much that the child grows up to be a citizen unable to manage their personal affairs.

A Much-Needed Reality Check

Have you ever thought why wealthy people like celebrities, industrialists, etc., send their children to school?

For instance, King Charles started his formal education at Hill House School in West London; Rajiv Gandhi, the former prime minister of India, went to The Doon school, Dehradun, India; and Abhishek Bachchan, the son of superstar Amitabh Bachchan, attended Jamnabai Narsee School and Bombay Scottish School in Mumbai and Modern School at Vasant Vihar, New Delhi. But why did their parents, despite having all the riches in the world to afford any home tutor, send their children to school? This is because schooling is one-fourth about education and three-fourths of it is about developing social skills. While education stimulates our intellectual abilities, there are certain skills that we learn *only* in a school: being responsible, teamwork, resilience, service to mankind, accepting others without judgement, adjustment, compassion and, most importantly, managing ourselves and accepting defeat and triumph with equal ease.

Holistic and experiential learning, teamwork, resilience building, inclusivity, adjustment and tolerance are catchy expressions to dish out in speeches, self-improvement books and even in school or college manifestos. But do we know how to implement these as parents? According to me, parents either don't understand them or, even if they do, they do not have the gumption to implement these ideas. Remember, charity begins at home and so does character building.

Life is not a bed of roses, and the earlier we understand it and deal with kids accordingly to make them resilient, the better it is for the kids and also for society at large. Some of the rudimentary problems of parenting are:

- **Always Protecting Kids:** Parents do not want their kids to get hurt. So, they do every little thing for their child. But this is not going to make him or her strong. Let him or her take decisions, make mistakes and sort it out on their own.

- **Frequent Praising:** Everyone likes to be praised, but if it becomes a habit, a kid will do nothing without receiving praise. No kid is perfect, and pointing out the mistakes and correcting them is also a parent's job. If all they do is praise, despite the kids being wrong, they will not be open to self-criticism. This will hamper their ability of self-improvement.
- **Fulfilling Unreasonable Demands:** All parents want to see their kids happy and enjoying their lives. So, they fulfil even the most unreasonable demands of their child. Prepare a child to face the reality that he or she will not always get what he or she wants and nothing comes for free. Also, teach them to handle deprivation too.

Is the Next Generation Resilient?

Bullies are everywhere—schools, colleges and even at workplaces. Parents and teachers can support and protect children from such people in school and, to some extent, during college days. However, will parents be able to help if their child gets a job and meet such people there? They will have to manage such situations and people on their own.

They may get hurt by a temperamental boss, who makes their life difficult all the time! If there is office politics and the child gets upset, will the parents go and tear apart the entire team of 50 people because their child cannot take pulls and pressures that they have not taken till date?

If a child has been brought up in an overprotective environment, where all their complaints and grievances were always addressed by their parents, their child will find it difficult to fight the world alone.

Who Should Read This

I have written this in a comprehensible way so that it is accessible to all kinds of people. If a child faces any difficulty in understanding the chapter, the parents can read it, explain the concept and encourage them to understand, absorb the idea and implement it when required. Once a child has used the concept, they must give feedback to their parents. This entire process has to become a habit in order to yield results.

Why This Book Is Different

This book is a practical approach—a tool—to teach you how to handle difficult people and difficult situations. You cannot change the world and the situations or the people you need to deal with every day. However, you can always learn to handle these effectively. This book is a guide on how to handle life's challenges.

IN A NUTSHELL

How to Read and Use the Book?

This book has stories with characters depicting different scenarios and situations in which a child can find themselves—mostly in schools. Each story has some lessons at the end that are easy to follow. The lessons have to be first understood and then applied as per the situation. This is, in a way, learning 'mental kung fu'.

1

What Is Bullying?

'I realized that bullying never has to do with you. It's the bully who's insecure.'

—Shay Mitchell,
American actress

In your day-to-day life, you meet, interact and deal with many people. Dealing with people is an art, which is essential for your survival. Out of all these people that you meet daily, there will be some who will habitually seek to harm you, intimidate you or try to dominate you; they are called bullies.

Bullies take pleasure in coercing and even tormenting others. Sometimes, such people can make your lives miserable, mentally and physically.

Characteristics of a Typical Bully

If you want to face your bully head-on, you must know their personality traits. For example, on a cricket pitch, a batsman tries to gauge the strengths and weaknesses of a bowler. He prepares himself accordingly for a spinner, a fast bowler or a bowler who is good at googly. Just like a batsman prepares himself accordingly for different bowlers to play well, it is important for us to prepare accordingly for different kinds of bullies to lead a peaceful life.

Therefore, it is necessary to understand the typical characteristics of a bully, which are:

- They have an inferiority complex and might want to compensate for it by showing off.
- They have an inflated ego.
- They have a tendency to dominate others.
- They have little empathy.
- They might have bullying parents or siblings.
- They are rowdy by nature.
- They take pride in the fact that others fear them.

Where Does Bullying Happen?

It can happen anywhere—schools, colleges, government offices or private institutions. It can be in the cafeterias, playgrounds, classrooms and even toilets. It can also happen outside the school, on the school bus or on the roadside. Bullying also happens in any place of socializing like discos, malls, libraries, etc.

Types of Bullying

Bullying can simply start with a joke and could escalate to name calling or even physical abuse.

A bully usually tests their ground. They check the capacity of the person they are bullying and how much they can push one before the person getting bullied either breaks down or retaliates. After testing the victim, the bullies take the following actions depending on the victim's vulnerability:

- **Mean Gestures:** These include making faces, jeering, teasing and using bad body language.
- **Social Exclusion:** Here, a group of bullies gets together and isolates an individual. The group makes sure that everyone around the victim stops responding and helping them. This is a way of psychological bullying.
- **Use of Violence:** Here, the bully attacks an individual in various situations. For instance, during a game of football or hockey, the bully can hurt someone during the game with the

hockey stick or hit them with the ball. Standing in a crowd, the bully can pinch one or pull their shirt to scare or annoy them. A bully can resort to using a stick, a ruler or even things like stones and bricks to hurt a person. In the worst cases, a bully can also use sharp objects like a knife to scare someone.

- **Mobbing:** Mobbing is an organized form of bullying. Here, six to eight people block one's way to bully them.
- **Extortion:** Here, a bully can push one over to pay them some money. The bully can also threaten to hurt them if they do not fulfil their demands. In school, a bully may trouble a student by snatching away their belongings.

The Games Bullies Play

A bully, according to me, always wants to 'appear stronger', but is actually insecure. Understanding this is the key to not being bullied. You should not give this impression to the bully that you are weak. Don't let the bully get pleasure out of troubling you. It is simple; if you do not react, the bully's efforts get wasted and they stop being a bother.

Here are four mind games that bullies play with their victims:

1. A bully always looks for a reaction from their victim. The more a victim cribs, the happier a bully is.
2. A bully looks for like-minded people for support and thrill while teasing the victim.
3. A bully targets an isolated individual.
4. Don't make it easy for the bully. To stop getting bullied, the bully should not know many things about you. One should not, in any scenario, reveal too much information about them.

Why Bullies Bully

According to psychologist Alfred Adler, superiority complexes are 'one of the ways which a person with an inferiority complex may use [as] a method of escape from his difficulties.'[1] A bully tries to show others that they are not inferior by posing to be superior and in control of things.

---

[1]Adler, Alfred, *Understanding Human Nature (Psychology Revivals)*, Routledge, 2013, p. 97.

IN A NUTSHELL

It is crucial to learn how to deal with bullies, and you should work on this right from your school days. Two things should be kept in mind to prevent getting bullied. First, do not react and ignore bullies. Never lose your sleep over a bully and do not take their words personally. Second, it is necessary to have a strong peer group of like-minded people whom you can trust. Your friends would be your safety shield—one for all and all for one.

2

Boost Your Self-Esteem and Self-Confidence

'Optimism is the faith that leads to achievement.
Nothing can be done without hope and confidence.'

—Helen Keller

The personality of a person can be gauged with their self-esteem. Low self-esteem is a feeling of being unimportant, unworthy and inept, leading to an overall lack of confidence. Bullying can be hurtful and can upset the victim so much that they constantly remain scared and start thinking of themselves as losers.

Research shows that children with low self-esteem

are more prone to bullying.[2] This chapter examines the ways to boost your self-esteem so that you do not succumb to bullying and emerge as stronger individuals. However, before diving into this, it is important to understand what exactly self-esteem means.

What Is Self-Esteem?

According to Merriam-Webster's dictionary, self-esteem is defined as 'a confidence and satisfaction in oneself'.

If one has low self-esteem, they always feel inferior to others, and subsequently, starts feeling miserable and unhappy. Therefore, one becomes an easy target of domination. Bullies may think, 'Oh, this guy! He has no confidence in himself. He appears to be weak and meek, so let us bully him.'

On the other hand, when one has a high self-esteem, they develop qualities that helps them navigate through the twisted manoeuvres of a bully. Therefore, it is important to develop self-confidence and self-esteem.

---

[2]'Effects of Bullying on Mental Health', *stopbullying.gov*, 25 October 2019, https://bit.ly/3nHTrqj. Accessed on 5 October 2023.

How to Develop Self-Confidence?

Developing self-confidence is not something that can happen overnight. Remember, Rome was not built in a day! You have to make conscious and steady efforts to make yourself a confident and a self-assured person. Remember, there may be moments when you won't feel confident, but that does not define you as an under confident person.

To become self-confident, you must strive to follow these 12 points:

1. **Read Motivational Books:** Reading books on motivation and leadership helps to improve one's confidence and give ideas to motivate oneself too.
2. **Read, Read and Read:** There is no better way to impress your peers other than radiating and disseminating knowledge. You must be so thorough with worldly wisdom that when you speak, people should lend their ears without a doubt. Hence, read as much as you can, be well-informed and have a cerebral approach towards various things.
3. **Making a List of Your Achievements:** There is not a single person who has not accomplished something small or big in life. Hence, it is important to make a list of these so that you get motivated by your accomplishments when you

look back at them. Your list of achievements can include small things too. For instance, helping an old lady cross a busy road may look like a small achievement, but it is surely something to be proud of. Listing these achievements will tell you about your personality—whether you are an empathetic person or a sociopath.

4. **Set Your Values Right:** This is extremely important if you want to succeed in life. You must be clear what you stand for. If one has no values, standards or ethics, then life has no meaning. If people are aware that an individual has a set of values to which they stick no matter what, people will respect and not fool around with that individual.
5. **Making Your Own Style Statement:** You need to create your own personality—an individual identity. Don't be a part of the herd if you want others to respect you and recognize you.
6. **Don't Pay Heed to What Others Say and Think:** Most of us don't take an initiative regarding something because we feel 'What will others think about me?' This is the biggest negative thing we can do to ourselves. Don't worry whether you succeed or fail. Just take the plunge.
7. **Don't Be Afraid of Failure:** You can never be confident if you suffer from 'what if' syndrome. If you think, 'Oh, what will happen if I fail?', you

will not be able to do anything and that is bad for your self-esteem. Do it without any fear. What may happen in the worst case? You may fail. But that is what life is all about.

8. **Look Good, Smell Good:** If you feel good about yourself, others will also start feeling that you are good. Also, putting forth a best version of yourself also helps to boost your confidence. Therefore, always dress up properly. Polish your shoes to look good, have bath every day and use some nice perfume to smell good. A well-groomed person leaves a lasting impression on others. It is also important to exercise, eat healthy food and look after your health to feel good and energetic.
9. **Company Matters:** You must choose your friends carefully. Many times, wrong company can ruin your life. In the context of self-esteem and morale, it is good to be with those who are enthusiastic and positive in outlook. Stay away from those who keep criticizing everything.
10. **Move On from Your Past:** We all make mistakes in life. Some people let these failures get the better of them. Move on. Don't let your past ruin your present and future.
11. **Learn from Your Mistakes:** You may make mistakes but don't repeat them. Always analyse where you went wrong and how you can improve.

12. **Become a Mentor and Help Others:** Sharing your knowledge with others can help you too. Once you teach others, you get more confident of your craft and feel proud that people are learning from you and respecting you. That makes you feel good and adds to your self-esteem. I had a student from Gwalior who used to provide tuitions when she was doing her graduation. She used to say that conducting classes built her confidence tremendously. No wonder she passed her MBA with flying colours.

Developing Your Personality

How can you leave a lasting impression on people within a short time? When you meet someone in a casual way or for a formal interview, an impression is formed about you within the first few minutes. Therefore, it is important to understand what is expected from you.

I have interviewed thousands of students as well as corporate executives. From those interactions, I have discerned that people who come for interviews are not aware of the basics. There are three basic dimensions of one's personality. This is not only for an interview but also applicable to social interactions as well.

1. **Appearance:** You should dress according to the occasion. If you are going for a formal meeting or an interview, make sure you wear appropriate clothes and look neat and tidy. Always remember, your first impression, is usually your last impression.
2. **Communication Skills:** Whenever you speak, make sure to shape your thoughts well. If you have time to prepare, write down your points. First, discuss the most important points and handle the lesser important ones later. Don't speak too fast, pause appropriately and let the other person understand your point before you move on to the next one. Whatever you are discussing must be clear in your mind, and you should be able to say it with confidence and absolute clarity. It is important to look into people's eyes when you speak. This makes a lasting impact. It is important to look cheerful and not glum faced. At appropriate occasions, you can smile too—it helps. Connect with the people on an emotional level by modulating your voice and using appropriate body language to express yourself. Rehearse in front of a mirror and see for yourself how you look.
3. **Knowledge:** This is where the grasp of the subject is important. In everyday life, you don't talk about physics or chemistry. You usually talk of subjects of

social interest. That is why, it is important to be wise in worldly affairs. To enhance your general knowledge, read newspapers, magazines and story books regularly.

IN A NUTSHELL

The more you meet and speak to people and participate in discussions with friends, the more confident you become. It is very helpful to listen to great speakers. Listen to interviews of successful people. The best way is to learn from others. Make sure you groom yourself and enhance your overall personality.

3

Develop Emotional Intelligence

'Not everything that can be counted counts and not everything that counts can be counted.'

—Albert Einstein

To be successful in all spheres of life, academic brilliance is not enough. Academics alone cannot get you respect of your peers and seniors.

Qualities like interpersonal skills, ability to accept failure, cooperative spirit, understanding other's emotions and hard work are equally important. All these qualities fall in the realm of EQ. While age may not be a bar while developing these qualities, it is easier to imbibe these when we are young.

Let us take the example of cricketer Sachin Tendulkar. He is a great batsman, extremely hard working, meticulous and can play under tremendous pressure. It is precisely for these reasons that he is respected by his co-players and even his competitors.

Just like him and many other successful people, you need to develop these skills to become successful and well-respected. It has been well proven that great confident leaders like J.R.D. Tata, Narayana Murthy and Azim Premji are successful not only because of their professional knowledge but also because of their qualities like strong willpower, love for their job, ability to handle failure, etc. These people also had a firm belief in values like honesty, integrity and caring for others. These humane qualities must be acquired by you and practised in day-to-day life to be different from the herd and have an edge over others.

Defining EQ

Since the beginning of the last century, as many of the discoveries and inventions were related to science, the study of sciences became important for our progress. Due to this, a lot of importance was given to science and technology and the concept of intelligence quotient(IQ) to test the logical reasoning ability came into being.

Gradually, we moved towards service-based economy, and employability options were more as compared to the time of manufacturing and industrial economy. The service economy in developing countries is mostly concentrated in financial services, hospitality, retail, health, human services, information technology and education. These required different skill sets than what was required in the industrial economy.

Managing rude customers, dealing effectively with teammates and colleagues, human interaction and interpersonal skills became more important than ever before. This brought the realization that besides science and technology, there are other more important skills required to work effectively. These were defined as emotional intelligence(EQ).

Besides IQ, an equally important ingredient for success is EQ. Qualities like commitment, honesty, caring for others and resilience to withstand pressure are therefore as essential for success as IQ. Emotional intelligence is a combination of these aforementioned qualities which makes us perform better than the best in any given field.

Therefore, whatever profession you choose, emotional intelligence is an essential requirement for success. Author and psychologist Daniel Goleman once said:

> 'If your emotional abilities aren't in hand, if you don't have self-awareness, if you are not able to manage your distressing emotions, if you can't have empathy and have effective relationships, then no matter how smart you are, you are not going to get very far.'[3]

Relation between EQ and Bullying

You may be academically brilliant but if you do not have the ability to stand up for yourself, bullies will take advantage of you. Hence, it becomes imperative to teach children how to deal with emotions and how to cultivate empathy.

This, in turn, helps them in building the characteristics of resilience and patience. In fact, children with higher emotional quotient are likely to be bullied less than those who have poor EQ.

Competencies Associated with EQ

According to Goleman, EQ has four aspects:

1. **Self-Awareness:** The first aspect of emotional intelligence is self-awareness. In fact, it is the bedrock

[3]Serrat, Olivier, *Knowledge Solutions: Tools, Methods, and Approaches to Drive Organizational Performance*, Springer Singapore, 2017, pp. 329–339.

of emotional intelligence. It helps you to realize and understand your strengths and weaknesses. Not just that, it helps to recognize your emotions and what effect they can have on you.

2. **Self-Management:** Self-management is the ability to manage your emotions, especially when it is triggered by stressful situations. The lack of self-management can lead people to evoke strong reactions, and also makes it hard for them to keep their impulses in check.
3. **Social Awareness:** Social awareness is your ability to acknowledge and reflect on the emotions and social cues of others. Reading situations is as important as understanding and managing your own emotions.
4. **Relationship Management:** It refers to your ability to influence, coach and mentor others and resolve conflict effectively.

Can EQ Be Improved?

Yes! First, we need to be aware of ourselves and accept our weaknesses without judgement. Having done that, we can start making small changes in our habits and gradually improve our EQ.

IN A NUTSHELL

Always look upto successful people and try to imbibe their qualities. Make sure you give equal importance to IQ and EQ. Read inspiring stories of people those who have done wonders against all odds.

4

Create a Buddy System

'Only by binding together as a single force will we remain strong and unconquerable.'

—Chris Bradford,
English author and martial artist

It is quite common to take time to get used to a new environment—a new home, a new town or a new school. When you join a new school, you will meet your new classmates. Some friendly, some shy, some helpful and some downright nasty. The last category belongs to those, who take pleasure in bullying others, insulting others and demeaning their classmates as well as their juniors in the school.

Having a 'Bully Repellant'

Some of the bullies are stronger than you and make you their target or a punching bag. You may not be able to handle such classmates alone as they can be overbearing and you may not be that brave to stand up against them. So, what is one supposed to do? How will you face the bullies head on? The answer lies in making friends; the more friends you have, the less the chances of getting bullied. Having a close friend is paramount in surviving the world. I call such a friend 'buddy'. Buddies have matching tastes, hobbies and interests to be buddies. You choose your buddy carefully from your larger friends' group.

Buddies take care of each other in more ways than one. They exchange class notes, inform the teacher of each other's well-being, spend time together, study together and play together. The biggest advantage is that with buddies, you are never alone, and, hence, bad guys can't corner you. A buddy becomes your partner in distress too; when someone tries to bully you, your buddy's presence is enough to dissuade a bully. You both act as a 'bully repellant' for each other.

A Story to Inspire Making a Buddy

Shrey had just changed his school. The idea was to move to a school that had a better reputation, academic atmosphere and infrastructure and facilities for students. Since he was good at studies and had a great academic track record right from the second standard, it was not difficult for him to get admission.

However, a change of environment can take a toll on the mental health of a young student, and Shrey was no different. He had come from a school where he had made several friends effortlessly, and all the teachers and the staff knew him well. The new school was huge and had several sections for every class; it was overwhelming for Shrey.

There were 40 students in his class. Mrs Sharma, the class teacher, was a strict disciplinarian. In his new class, he also met Mridula, the class monitor. She was nice, had a pleasant personality and was mature for her age. She introduced Shrey to Umang, Raj and Kunal so that he could have some buddies. They were all nice and decent. Within a week, he was comfortable and well-adjusted in the environment. Out of the three, he found Kunal to be the best. He was cheerful, had a good sense of humour and was also regular with his studies.

They both sat on the same bench and spent a lot of time together during the breaks too. Both of them liked reading story books and comics—that was their common interest. Fortunately, they stayed in the same colony and took the same school bus home every day. They also met in the evenings to play football in the public park. Shrey found Kunal to be a helpful person in every aspect. Soon, they became close friends and shared their problems and academic difficulties with each other too. Their parents also became friends and both spent time at each other's place. Once or twice, Shrey went to spend a whole day at Kunal's place. It was a great experience as they saw some TV programmes together and talked a lot. It was very different from school time.

While things were good at home, their school was a different story. In their class, they would come across some rowdy students. Among such students, Vishal was the worst. He would call himself a Dada, i.e., a big boss, or a baddy. His parents were called several times by Mrs Sharma and counselled by her to ensure that Vishal worked hard in studies and attended classes regularly, but nothing worked. Vishal was neither good at studies nor at games or any extra curricular activity. His favourite pastimes were to while away time and tease other classmates. He also bullied those who were smaller than him or meek in behaviour. Since he had nothing better to do, he would get hold of someone and try to trouble him. If someone was a little overweight, he would often fat shame them. If he found anyone speaking against him, he would not hesitate to bully them physically. No one liked him.

One day, as Shrey was walking alone, Vishal came from the opposite side. As Vishal came close to him, he put his arm around Shrey's smaller frame and said nastily, 'Hey smally, have you been complaining about me to Madam Sharma and class monitor Mridula? Don't try to cross me if you want to survive, bro.' Shrey froze with fear and replied, 'But I never complained to anyone. Please leave me alone.' Vishal squeezed Shrey's arm, shook him badly and said loudly, 'You don't know me as yet and I don't spare anyone who crosses my path.'

Suddenly, they heard someone saying, 'Oh, so you are trying to trouble my best friend? Okay, let me see what you can do to him.' It was Kunal. Shrey was relieved and struggled to free his arm from Vishal. At Kunal's arrival, Vishal started looking around for an escape route meekly. He knew that they were best friends and he alone would not be a match for both of them. He ran away quickly. Both Kunal and Shrey laughed out loud. Shrey said, 'Thank you, Kunal. I was very scared until you came along.'

Kunal replied nonchalantly, 'Shrey, we are best friends. After all, what is the point of having friends if we can't be there for them at the hour of their need? After all, a friend in need is friend indeed.' This was a great lesson for Shrey, and he shared this incident with others in the class. Now, all boys and girls realized the power of friends and quickly organized themselves into buddies, never to be caught alone by rogues like Vishal.

IN A NUTSHELL

Try to maintain a friendship like Shrey and Kunal with whom you share common interests and try to find like-minded people to be friends with. A true friend will always stand by you and you do not have to fear getting bullied.

5

Team Up for the Effect

'Teamwork is the fuel that allows common people to attain uncommon results.'

—Andrew Carnegie,
American industrialist and philanthropist

Teamwork is extremely important to handle bullies or troublemakers. That is why, even in a jungle, the prey, if alone, is singled out by the predator! Similarly, if humans stay together, they are safe.

A Story on the Importance of Teamwork

Rakesh Saxena, a banker by profession, was recently transferred from Chennai to Delhi. His son Akshay, who was in ninth grade, had joined a new school. He was good at studies and was an all-rounder, taking part in drama and sports alike. Within a month, he was liked by his teachers and the principal. They identified his potential in a school debate where he won the first prize. He was a good kid who mostly kept to himself as he was a little introvert by nature.

His success did not go down well with Kailash, who was in the same class and had been in the same school for the last 10 years. Son of a rich businessman, Kailash had a lot of airs about himself. He loved being called Kally as it sounded cool to him. He had money to spend and had a few sidekicks who were happy to live off his parents' money. He used to show off his expensive mobile, watches and sunglasses. When he would pass by, one could not miss a whiff of some expensive cologne or perfume.

Heavily built, he was a rowdy boy. Even seniors did not dare mess with him. Since he was neither good at studies nor at any sport, he used to satisfy his ego by bullying other students from the school. Although there were constant complaints against him, he did not mend his ways. Akshay was aware about this and, therefore, kept away from this guy. Kailash didn't like this and wanted to teach him a lesson to ensure Akshay bends and bows in front of him. Kally thought that Akshay was trying to be too big for his boots.

One day, when Akshay was sitting alone in the class during lunch break, Kailash, with his two sidekicks, barged in and said, 'Hi Akshay, we plan to bunk classes after the lunch break to see a movie. I want you to come along with us.' Akshay was taken aback but quickly replied, 'Kailash, I don't want to miss my classes. You all go ahead. I think it is not a good idea and you should also not bunk, you may get caught.' One of his sidekicks put his hand on Akshay's shoulder and said 'Boss, Kally is being decent with you and no one says no to him in the entire school. Do you know what he can do to you if you go against his wish?' Ignoring his thinly veiled threat, Akshay brushed aside his hand from his shoulder and walked out of the classroom. Kailash barked, 'This is not good for you, you sissy!' Akshay didn't respond.

The very next day, Kailash was back to his tricks. Akshay found a small chit on his desk, 'Hi sissy, I am asking you again? Want to come or not?' During the recess break they teased him by saying loudly in front of the whole class, 'Here goes the *darpok billee* [scaredy-cat]. What a saint, following all the rules, as if we are all punks.' Akshay felt humiliated and these torturous remarks only increased by the day. Though his classmates could see the tension written clearly on his face, none came to his rescue.

Akshay then realized that all the classmates knew

him but he had no close friends. He understood that to develop close friendships, he needed to spend quality time with people. His buddies would be the friends, who would come to his rescue when he faces any problem.

After giving some thought to the matter at hand, he identified a few classmates who could be trusted and be helpful. Within a week, he spoke to almost a dozen such students from his class and shared his concern about Kally and his sidekicks. All of them were aware of his tactics but none had the courage to stand up to him. At some point or the other, they were also victims of his bullying.

They now decided to make a group to handle this menace. Akshay advised them not to resort to any violence or become abusive as that would go against them. They decided that they would be firm and definitive in their stance instead. They took the initiative and met Kally outside the canteen. When he saw a dozen boys and girls approaching, he was surprised and a little scared too. Swati, one of the girls, spoke, 'Look Kailash, we have come here to tell you something. We want to tell you that we will not be mute spectators to your activities anymore and will not let it pass.'

In a tone of finality, Akshay added, 'We are all there for each other. Also, please understand, you will not bully anyone else from other classes either. This applies to your sidekicks also.'

Kailash was stunned at this and did not have the guts to look into their eyes. Rashmi, another victim of Kailash's bullying stated, 'Kailash, please don't try to isolate anyone and brow beat them. From now on, no one is alone. We are all for one and one for all.'

This simple conversation was so impactful that every group member was also surprised with the result that followed. Next day onwards, Kally and his sidekicks started behaving properly and, within a week all the bitterness evaporated. He started to be sweet to make up for his stupidities in the past.

IN A NUTSHELL

If you make a small team with a well-defined goal, it can work wonders. This is true not only in school or college but this habit is at the core of teamwork all throughout your life. So, learn to team up.

TEAM = **Together Everyone Achieves More**

6

Learn to Become Strong

'When the going gets tough, the tough get going.'

—A Popular Idiom

As has been reiterated, life is becoming more and more difficult. Though we have better technology, more comforts and better medical care, the environment is getting worse. People are getting intolerant, becoming frustrated, and on top of it, there are people who get sadistic pleasure in making your already difficult life more miserable.

You must be ready to fight against these bullies.

A Story on Fitness and Confidence

Vineet was an above-average student but not an extroverted fellow. He had a short goatee beard which he kept on fiddling whenever he was nervous. Rakesh and Manoj, two of his classmates, would take a dig at him several times in front of everyone and bully him. 'Oh weakling, you can do nothing in life, you are a loser.' These words pricked him. He did not want to pick a fight as he felt he was not strong enough compared to them. As a result, Vineet continued getting bullied by them. Surjit Singh, a student of twelfth grade and Vineet's senior, was a diligent student. He had cracked the National Defense Academy (NDA) exam and was felicitated by the principal of the school, Sachin Sharma.

Surjit, like Vineet, was not great at socializing. Hence, despite being a good student, he didn't stand out among his classmates. As a result, after the felicitation programme, some of the boys from Surjit's class teased and taunted him: 'This skinny fellow wants to join the Army, look at his thin legs and how silly he looks.' Used to these taunts, Surjit learnt to avoid them, but Vineet felt bad for Surjit. He went to him after school hours and said, 'Don't feel bad, they are just jealous of you. I am sure these guys can never crack such a tough exam in a lifetime. Thousands appear and only few make it to the merit list. I wish you good luck.' Surjit thanked him and left. At the end of June, Surjit went to Pune, where the academy was located.

It was a huge academy spread over more than 7,000 acres. He could have never imagined such a grand monumental place where he was to spend his next three years consisting of six terms. All of them were issued uniforms for various activities: working dress, physical training (PT) dress, battle dress, etc. Sikhs were given blue turbans. Surjit, in his uniform, looked smart and was proud to see himself in the mirror with his turban given by the academy with an NDA crest—*Service Before Self*—written on it.

The going was tough both in terms of academics and physical activities. Here, Surjit saw the power of camaraderie. There were more than 300 cadets in his batch, including army, air force and navy. The curriculum of the first four terms were same for all. There was also a lot of emphasis on physical fitness, sports and horse riding. The NDA had many thoroughbred horses. In Delhi, Surjit had seen horses only pulling *tangas* whereas these horses were well-built and really tall! He felt scared mounting a horse for the first time but gradually gained confidence. Drill was a part of the training where all the cadets marched in unison as a squadron.

Drills made each one stand straight, and there was no room for slouching. After a few months, their demeanour changed. They were much more fit, disciplined, smart and sharp. This training was a perfect grooming process for the young ones. There were boxing matches, athletics, hockey, volleyball and football competitions too.

Surjit was slowly yet steadily transforming through this process. He, who had never run in his life, was now running cross-country regularly and cycling at least 40 km a day because cadets had to use cycles to go and attend classes. Within months, he had strong legs and arms and acquired fine flexibility. He attained a military-like posture. Running 5–6 km was a cakewalk by now!

Six months went by in a jiffy. It was time for the winter break, which, for Surjit, was a time for a brief visit to his home and meeting his family that was equally eager to meet him.

As Surjit reached Delhi, his parents and brothers were happy to see him. They were also immensely surprised by his physical and psychological changes. 'You look smart, bro,' said Harjit, his younger brother.

The next day, Surjit went to his school with a box of sweets for the principal and his classmates. Most of the guys could not believe their eyes. A smart sardar wearing a beautifully tied red turban, an NDA scarf and a blazer with a silver NDA crest, Surjit looked confident in his appearance. He looked healthy and fit as a fiddle. Vineet also went to meet Surjit. 'You have completely changed,' he exclaimed.

He noticed respect and awe for his senior Surjit in the eyes of those who were earlier bullying him. 'Why can't I become as strong and smart as Surjit?' he thought. Next day, Vineet made a visit to Surjit's house. He asked, 'Can you give me tips so that I can become as strong and smart as you?'

Surjit took him out to the veranda. 'Look bro, there are no tips, it is all a result of hard work and training. I can train you with basics that I learnt at the NDA only if you want. However, you have to continue that regimen for several months, even after I return to the academy. Do you think you are ready? I am here for six weeks and will be exercising daily. You can join me if you want.' An excited Vineet replied, 'I am ready!'

Vineet's training started the very next day at 6.00 a.m. Surjit took him for a 2-km run. It was tough for Vineet.

'Sir, how do you manage this? I am panting and you look so relaxed after the run.'

Surjit said, 'Friend, this doesn't happen overnight. We were made to do this every day for almost three months before we could run a full-fledged NDA cross-country—about 8 km at a stretch across hills and jungles! Be at it and you will also get there in a while. Now, let's do some push-ups.'

He got on his fours on the road itself and did 50 at a stretch. Vineet could manage to do only five. The next day, Vineet reported for the training session, although his body was in immense pain. Surjit said, 'To remain fit, you need to work out regularly. I will ramp up the sessions gradually. Just don't give up.' Vineet replied, 'I won't give up at any cost.'

Surjit knew exactly what was going on in Vineet's mind. He had come to seek his help on purpose. He wanted to be strong so that he could stand against Manoj and Rakesh and their gang of bullies.

Surjit, who had gone through the NDA grind, said to Vineet 'I understand where you are coming from. You, like me, have been bullied and now you want to change that. Don't worry, I will do my best.' He assured him as an elder brother would.

Within 15 days, Vineet was clocking a good time and could run 4 km non-stop. He felt energetic after exercise. As time passed by, Surjit gave him some more tips to smarten up. 'Vineet, shave off your beard and polish your shoes every day. Take pride in your school uniform, wear your school tie properly and change the frame of your glasses. Use good talcum powder and smell nice.'

The physical training was almost over and Surjit had to return to the academy soon, and their join training sessions were almost over. 'Don't forget, Vineet, when the going gets tough, the tough get going. You need to do this on your own every day after I leave. Join a gym so that you train well and build your strength. Take only one-day break in a week, okay? I will be in touch regularly. Keep me updated every week.' Vineet affirmed in a confident tone. It was a delight for Surjit to witness the changes in him. Vineet joined a gym near his colony and continued with his exercise daily. He could feel the physical and mental transformation.

By now, Vineet felt stronger and more confident. Slowly, his classmates started noticing these changes too. After weeks of extensive and regular exercise, one day, he went to school with a clean-shaven face, polished shoes and a proper haircut. All the students in the class turned their heads and were pleasantly surprised to look at a new Vineet. However, Manoj and Rakesh didn't like all the glory and attention being showered on Vineet. To show him his place, Manoj put his hand around Vineet's shoulder to cow him down. This time, Vineet was ready. He refused to give in to Manoj's bullying, and one strong shove from Vineet made Manoj realize his mistake. Seeing Vineet's courage, Rakesh backed off. Vineet was finally able to stand up against his bullies.

That day, after returning home, he wrote a thank you note to Surjit. Surjit was happy for Vineet and wrote back to him. He advised Vineet to never give up and dig his heels in at all times. Vineet had become a strong and confident boy. He started participating in sport and games too.

Thanks to Surjit, no one could push Vineet around for life.

IN A NUTSHELL

As Ralph Waldo Emerson said, 'The only person you are destined to become is the person you decide to be.' It is, therefore, important to decide what you want to be, how you visualize yourself and then work on it. To face life's challenges, physical fitness is a game changer. Make it a habit for life. Feel fit and feel good.

7

Target Denial and Seeking Help

'Courage is fire, and bullying is smoke.'

—Benjamin Disraeli,
writer and British statesman

The best defence, in case of bullying, is 'target denial'. This simply means denying the bully any opportunity to make someone a target. In effect, target denial involves leaving a situation or circumstance that one deems unsafe. This act is also seen as one of the wisest decisions to be taken in such a situation.

A Story about Target Denial to Tackle Bullies

Surinder, a smart and fast learner, had recently joined a new school. In his previous school, his class teacher Miss Seema Kaul had taken a special interest in teaching how to tackle bullying. As Surinder came to this new school, he kept those teachings in mind and applied them at appropriate occasions. He knew that his class teacher's lessons were very useful.

The first lesson Surinder learnt was to move away from the people who were trying to bully him. In the new school, he had few friends. He could also identify the rogue elements in his class—Hari and Rajiv. They were the miscreants who would trouble new students the most.

One day, as Surinder was walking in the long corridor of the school, he noticed Hari standing next to a pillar. He knew that Hari would pass some silly remarks on seeing him. However, he was mentally prepared to handle the situation. He quickly recalled the role-play that was conducted by Miss Kaul in his previous school, and he was ready to execute that to protect himself from Hari.

Hari was much taller than Surinder and as the latter walked closer to Hari, his heart started pounding faster. He remembered how his teacher told him that this was a normal reaction of the body and he should keep a check on his emotions and fear. Surinder, as per the teachings of Miss Kaul, collected himself and said, 'Okay Hari, see you later. I am getting late for my next class. Bye,' and walked confidently past Hari pretending as if nothing happened. Before Hari could react, Surinder was about 15 yards away, well out of Hari's reach. His role-play came in handy and he emerged as a winner. Hari did not know how to react in such a situation and had a blank expression on his face. He said to himself, 'Surinder is quite a cool guy.'

Two weeks later, Surinder was confronted by Rajiv—another bully from his class—near the school canteen. A lot of students were present there as it was the recess time. From Rajiv's body language, Surinder understood that Rajiv was going to take a dig at him—possibly in an aggressive manner. Rajiv came close to him, said something nasty and shoved Surinder hard. Surinder knew that the situation was different and that he could not move away like he had done in the corridor with Hari. 'Time to apply another tactic,' he thought. Surinder again referred to Miss Kaul's teachings to handle such a situation. He was advised in the previous school that if the victim yells loudly when people are around, a bully would develop cold feet and retreat.

Surinder put both his hands in front and shouted: 'Stop! Go away! Friends, please help! Call the teacher. Rajiv is hurting me.' This was enough as everyone around looked at the scenario and stared at Rajiv. Embarrassed at the situation, Rajiv retreated and rushed back to his class. Rajiv understood that he could not mess with Surinder again.

As Rajiv was leaving, one of Surinder's classmates said, 'Surinder, that was cool. We have all learnt a lesson that we need to stand up for ourselves in such a situation and seek the help of friends. We also learnt that bullies are cowards and can never face public humiliation. Thanks, bro, I think you did a great job.'

Surinder's courage and presence of mind became the talk of the town. Everyone praised Surinder for taking a stand against the bully.

That evening, when Surinder returned home, he shared this experience with his parents. They were glad that their son handled the situation tactfully. The incident was also discussed with his younger sister Sarita so that she could also learn the lesson well and, if required, use it if she experienced bullying.

IN A NUTSHELL

Sun Tzu (400–320 BC), the Chinese general and military theorist, in his book *The Art of War* wrote, 'To win one hundred victories in one hundred battles is not the acme of skill. To subdue the enemy without fighting is the acme of skill.'[4] To tactfully avoid the enemy, or a bully in our case, is the best way to manage a situation. You simply avoid confrontation, and it leaves the bully totally dejected as the person did not get an opportunity to harass or trouble you. Remember, a bully wants to get a reaction from you; they feel thrilled seeing you get harassed. Hence, avoid the bully and don't give the person that chance.

[4]Sun Tzu, *The Art of War*, Samuel. B Griffith (trans.), Oxford University Press, 1963, p. 77.

8

Handle Your Emotions and Fears

'Bravery is the capacity to perform properly even when scared half to death.'

—Omar N. Bradley,
US army general

Fear is a state of mind. We sometimes overthink the scale or magnitude of the difficulty. Hence, in some situations, we get more scared than we should be. Taking deep breaths when you are tensed in a situation is a helpful trick to sail through the problem. If your heart starts beating faster or you have sweaty palms, the best thing is to stay where you are, place your palm on your stomach and breathe slowly.

The goal is to help your body and mind understand that there is nothing to fear.

A Story on Controlling Emotions

Rahul was in ninth grade and had turned out to be quite mature in his outlook. His father was in the army and, therefore, Rahul had to change schools every three-to-four years. Some army kids have a negative impact because of these frequent transfers but Rahul took these changes in a positive light. He was able to adapt to different environment and different cultures. In fact, it was quite a useful experience that helped him to evolve emotionally.

His father always said, 'Fear is in your mind and if you can tide over that moment of fear, you are called brave.'

Rahul had learnt to face his fears from his parents at an early age.

His father narrated a story to him of Field Marshal Sam Manekshaw, who had been awarded the Military Cross for bravery in war. He had taken a hit of several bullets in his stomach during action. He was popularly called Sam Manekshaw, or even Sam Bahadur.

His father told him about an incident when Sam Bahadur, during World War II, was a Major commanding a Charlie Company. His father said that

Sam Bahadur faced a crisis when the Commanding Officer sought to promote Surat Singh, who was a troublemaker. Sam Bahadur vehemently objected to this choice. Later, Surat Singh threatened to shoot him due to that rejection, resulting in his arrest and a potential death penalty.

Sam Bahadur confronted him, loading his pistol himself, and challenged Surat Singh to shoot Sam Bahadur if he had the courage. Surat Singh apologized, and Sam Bahadur took a bold step by assigning him to guard his tent overnight. Surat Singh did nothing from then on and he became a loyal and obedient soldier.[5]

Rahul was inspired by this story. One day, he faced a bully in his class called Prabir. Prabir always troubled Rahul and used to beat him up to show his power in the class. Prabir was a burly tall guy and there was no way Rahul could defeat him in a fight. He was scared to the bones but was reminded of his father's lessons and the story of Sam Manekshaw.

He faced Prabir, who was waiting under a tree like a lion looking for its prey. Prabir was staring at him. 'Now is the time to be brave,' thought Rahul.

---

[5]Sam Manekshaw spoke of this incident in a lecture at Defence Service College, Wellington, on 11 Novermber 1998. See: 'Sam Manekshaw on Leadership and Discipline', *IDR Indian Defence Review,* 4 August 2023, https://tinyurl.com/3uf7ct5b, Accessed on 12 October 2023.

He looked straight at Prabir as if treating him as an equal if not inferior. Prabir, who was expecting Rahul to be scared, was taken aback and didn't utter a word. Rahul's tactics worked and as he reached his class, he was proud of himself.

When he reached home, he narrated the incident to his father. Happy to know that his son was able to handle the situation appropriately, he looked at him proudly and said, 'Look! You did it, and I had told you that if you can handle that moment of fear with your chin up, you emerge as a winner. I am proud of you, Rahul.'

Next week, Harshad, another bully notorious for jeering at students, almost confronted Rahul in the school cafeteria. Rahul wore spectacles and Harshad took a dig on his spectacles and said in front of everyone in the canteen, 'You four-eyed goat, can you even see the blackboard in the class? Your glasses are so thick, I am sure you are as good as blind.' Rahul was hurt but remembered the lesson he received during one of the briefings on bullying by his class teacher in the previous school. She had said to him, 'In a situation when someone insults you, it is better to disregard that remark and move on as if nothing has happened. There is no point in arguing or showing that you are hurt because a bully wants you to feel hurt and they are not prepared to listen to any logic.'

Therefore, Rahul walked away with dignity and paid no heed to Harshad at all. Harshad got pissed off because he was expecting a reaction from Rahul, but Rahul defeated him at his own game.

IN A NUTSHELL

Fear is a necessary evil and no one is really fearless. However, you need to control yourself when you are in a situation that scares you. It could be a dark area or a bully. If you keep imagining that bully to be Goliath or Frankenstein's monster, you will get more scared. However, if you do not let these control you, you can control yourself, just like Rahul.

9

Learn to Fight Back

'The last three or four reps is what makes the muscle grow. This area of pain divides a champion from someone who is not a champion.'

—Arnold Schwarzenegger

Instead of always looking for help, you must learn to fight your own battles. When you team up with well meaning friends who are strong and helpful, you become motivated to be like them. Gaining physical strength is important for your self-defence and also makes you confident to face bullies.

A Story on the Importance of Physical Fitness

When Vinayak, who hailed from Jaipur, entered eighth grade, he was physically unfit and had grown an uneven and unimpressive stubble. Owing to his haggard look, he came across as weak and a pushover to his peers. As a result, he became the perfect target for any aggressive bully. Baljeet, Sandeep and Arun were the notorious bullies of their class and would take a dig at Vinayak whenever they got an opportunity.

One day, Arun said, 'Look at his face and his teeth. No girl will ever speak to him, forget about kissing him.' These daily taunts and barbs were infuriating for a boy on the brink of puberty, but Vinayak felt helpless as he did not have the guts to retaliate. He was quite fed up with them but could do little as he thought of himself as weak.

On the contrary, Balwant, his elder brother, was athletically built. While Vinayak was lazy and didn't take part in sports at all, Balwant was a fitness enthusiast, part of almost every school sports team and also the captain of their school cricket team. He was, in fact, one of the few fast-paced bowlers of the school and was respected and praised by everyone in his class. Whenever he entered the school cafeteria, heads would turn. Though he was not aggressive by nature, he was often hailed as 'Big Brother'.

About a year ago, Balwant had been adjudged 'Mr Jaipur' in a bodybuilding competition. He had worked hard for this, and Vinayak used to see him practising at home on parallel bars that he had installed in the house's open courtyard. He would do push-ups with just a bench and a couple of bricks. Balwant had also joined a gym but he had made sure that his passion didn't negatively impact his academic performance. Balwant would take every opportunity to do some exercise, would go for a mile or two to jog in the morning before having his breakfast.

Vinayak had been impressed on seeing his brother sweat and toil to become fit. 'I wish I could be like Balwant,' he thought. One day, he mustered up the courage and went to Balwant when he was studying for his exams. He asked softly, 'Can I speak to you for a minute?'

'Of course. What is troubling you, Vinayak? You seem lost and perturbed,' he asked with genuine concern in his eyes.

A hesitant Vinayak asked, 'Can I also build a body like yours?'

Hearing his question, Balwant couldn't be happier that his brother finally wanted to look after his health. 'Why not! But, are you prepared to work hard? You've heard of the old adage, "no pain, no gain", right?' He asked.

Taking his words to heart, Vinayak said, 'Yes, I will do whatever it takes.'

'Okay, done. Let's start from tomorrow. I will fix up a gym membership with Sameer. He owns a gym.'

'But why can't I practise at home with you? Why a gym? Is it necessary?' asked Vinayak.

'Vinayak, a gym is like a temple where you religiously go to work out. It is the best way to maintain discipline in exercise. A gym provides you not only with the necessary equipment but also gives you a serious environment where lots of like-minded people come to work out. I will get you a good trainer who can design the curriculum for you and help you work out properly for better results.'

During his first day at the gym, Vinayak was in awe of the infrastructure. 'Wow, it looks so cool,' he thought. It was a gym spread over 5,000 sq.ft and had ropes, pullies, sandbags and weights arranged neatly. There was a boxing ring as well. Balwant introduced Vinayak to his gym instructor. 'Vinayak, meet Rampal. He will be your trainer.' Although Rampal looked burly, he was polite and professional in his behaviour.

Looking at the instructor, Vinayak felt a bit overwhelmed. 'Today, I feel I will get scolded,' thought Vinayak.

However, he was surprised when Rampal said,

'Vinayak, I assume you do not play any outdoor games and have never worked out till now, right?'

Feeling a little embarrassed, Vinayak said, 'Yes, that is right.'

Vinayak knew he wasted a lot of time in a day playing video games. Rampal smiled and said, 'There is a first time for everything. Don't worry, we shall go slow and steady. You cannot become healthy in a day. It is a long journey, but a journey of thousand miles starts with a single step.'

Vinayak was impressed with Rampal's approach.

'Always remember,' Rampal continued, 'consistency is the key to success and becoming fit. If you are regular, listen to what I say and do exactly as you are told, I can assure you that you can transform yourself into a healthier and fitter person.'

Encouraged by his words, Vinayak said, 'Yes, sir. I am ready for this.'

Rampal laughed and said, 'Please don't call me sir, just Rampal will do.' Vinayak nodded and began his journey with a deep breath.

Rampal said, 'The first rule you must learn when it comes to working out is that you need to warm up before every session. Without warm-up, you will hurt yourself.'

Thus, they started with a little warm-up. In the first 10 minutes, Rampal taught Vinayak some simple exercises, mostly jogging and cardio. In those 10 minutes, Vinayak began to sweat and pant.

'Now relax for 60 seconds,' said Rampal. Then, they started with squats and exercises for legs and the core.

One hour flew by and Vinayak shook hands, thanked Rampal and returned home on his cycle. He felt light and happy.

He was physically tired but mentally energized. At home, after having a banana shake and a hearty dinner, he went off to sleep. The next day, he felt his entire body aching. He could barely get out of his bed. However, he didn't forget his promise and did his morning chores with sheer willpower, got ready and rode his cycle to school.

'Oh god! Every muscle in my body is aching,' he thought. Despite the tremendous pain, he reached the gym timely.

Within a week, he got used to his new routine. He looked forward to his sessions with Rampal every day. It was like an addiction. He was now lifting weights, flipping big tires and climbing ropes as well. Though the sessions were tough, with each day being a notch higher, he enjoyed every minute of it.

Any instructor or a gym trainer first examines the pupil for a week or so to ascertain the basic threshold of his abilities and the pupil's level of commitment before starting serious work out. By now, Rampal was convinced that Vinayak was dead serious and would be able to take the rigour and not drop out after a month or so. He saw that commitment in his eyes. Once there was a will, there was a way.

Therefore, after a week or so, Rampal asked Vinayak a crucial question: 'Tell me, Vinayak. What do you want from this workout? What is your purpose?'

Vinayak was very clear about his requirement: 'Rampal, I want a good physique. I want to look and feel good about myself. I want to earn respect from people.'

Rampal smiled and said, 'I am impressed. You are clear on your goals. Let me introduce you to Shalini, who is our professional dietician. She will guide you on what to eat and how much to eat to achieve your goals. Meanwhile, I will design your workout plan.'

Shalini made a fantastic diet plan for Vinayak. She included a balance of carbs, protein and fat so that he could build muscles. Within a few months of following the diet and the workout plan, Vinayak could flip huge tires and do bench presses. Throwing sandbags weighing 40 kg over the shoulders had become a child's play for him by then.

Over time, his stamina improved. His appetite was at an all-time high and he felt energetic the whole day. He also began to sleep soundly thus getting the required eight hours of sleep.

To motivate himself further, he started watching sports channels, borrowed some books on fitness from Rampal only to delve deep into the science of fitness.

After six months of rigorous training, Vinayak felt like a new person. People around him, including his classmates, began to notice changes in his physique.

Just to take his exercise regimen to the next level, he bought a thick rope and tied it to the tree outside their home. He and Balwant then climbed up the 30-ft rope at least twice a day just for fun. By now, his bullies had automatically backed off. They knew that even three of them would not be able to take on Vinayak.

One evening, Vinayak, along with his gym partner and classmate Rita, was returning home from gym, when two boys suddenly confronted them and one of them passed a lewd remark on Jasleen. She felt humiliated. Vinayak, unable to take this, went up to the boy and reprimanded him for his actions. The boy pushed Vinayak back, and in a split second, Vinayak caught hold of him by his collar and pushed him back. Even Vinayak was surprised by his own action.

Scared and helpless, the boy said, 'Sorry friend, I made a mistake.' Vinayak just dropped him like a dead weight.

'Next time, if I see you jokers around, I will bash you up right and proper,' snarled he.

Next day, Vinayak was the talk of the town as Jasleen narrated this incident to her friends. Baljeet, Arun and Sandeep walked up to him and shook hands, saying, 'We are glad that you could protect Jasleen. Our class is proud of you.'

Instantly, Vinayak thought of other boys in the school who were also the victims of bullying. He thought of helping them out. He requested Jasleen to prepare a list and, lo and behold, he could identify about 15 students who were being bullied constantly. One day, he called all of them during the recess. They all gathered under the famous banyan tree that was there.

He said, 'I know you people are being bullied by some of your classmates. I want to help you and will do the best I can. However, you need to stand up for yourself too. Next time, someone bullies you, please let me know and I will make sure that it never happens again.'

However, Vinayak could not be present everywhere at the same time. So, he worked out a strategy. He roped in five more students from the school football team, three from boxing and three from the 15 who were being bullied. Of course, Vinayak was the leader.

Vinayak had become bully-buster for these boys and, in no time, he became popular for his heroic acts. He was so proud and thought, 'Once I was so scared, and today, I am helping others. I did it!'

IN A NUTSHELL

Going to a gym, lifting weights and sweating it out can never be dangerous if done under proper supervision. You have great return on your investment; you become fitter and healthier and not a pushover. Moreover, you also become an example who can motivate others.

10

Exercise Cyber Intelligence

'Cyber-bullying is poised to turn into the biggest online concern, already affecting up to 35% of all children.'

—Dr Martyn Wild,
cyber safety expert

Technology makes our lives easier and helps in the advancement of generations. We have, for example, built powerful vehicles, huge factories and skyscrapers, dams and cities. However, this advancement comes at a terrifying cost. For instance, all the above examples of technological advancement comes at the cost of destroying our climate.

Similarly, the Internet has made our life comfortable. We can buy goods online, communicate with friends across the world via mails, and chat and make new friends on social media. The flip side of this is scary. Bank accounts have been hacked due to cyber frauds, manipulative games that take lives of people—the list goes on.

Online predators look for vulnerable youth, pretends to be someone else, try to gain the trust of an individual and then attempt cyberbullying. It is important *not* to accept a friend request or communicate with someone on social media who is not personally known to you. One of the most consistently found differences between traditional bullying and cyberbullying is that victims can be bullied anytime from anywhere because most children have access to digital devices outside of school. It only takes one click to ruin a kid's life.

Types of Cyberbulling

Before we get into the nuances of cyberbullying, it is important to understand the different types of it. This enables you to be aware and not become a victim of cyberbullying. Some of these are:

- Issuing online threats, thereby provoking an individual to kill themselves or hurt someone else

- Triggering religious, racial, ethnic or political vitriol online by posting hate comments
- Faking an identity online to ask for an indecent picture
- Posting fake information and hurtful rumours about an individual online
- Publishing a photoshopped photo or video
- Creating a fake or inappropriate webpage about another individual

A Story on Doxing

The story below is an example of doxing. 'Dox' means to stalk and publish private information about a particular individual on the Internet, typically with malicious intent.

Trisha was good with computers and pretty savvy with her smartphone too. She had thousands of friends on her social media account. In fact, she would blindly accept all friend requests without bothering to check their profiles. She changed her profile picture every week and posted everything she did. She was often told by her friends that her habit of accepting every random friend request would land her in trouble, but their words would always fall on deaf ears.

One day, as she checked her messages on her social media account, she found a message from an unknown account that read: 'I know what you did. I know who you are. I am going to follow you like your shadow and will expose you soon' along with an inappropriate, photoshopped image of hers. Trisha trembled with fear. She realized that someone had been stalking her online. 'How stupid of me to post everything online!' she cried.

She quickly logged on to her laptop and deleted all her pictures from her social media accounts. She realized that she should have done this earlier and should have never shared everything online.

The next day, she opened her smartphone only to have another message, 'You think I am dumb! You cannot remove your digital footprint from the virtual world. I already have all the data with me, and I will show you what I can do. I will ruin your life.'

She shivered. At the same time, she was angry with everything that was happening, and, on an impulse, wanted to give a fitting reply. However, better sense prevailed. 'If I respond, the bully will be delighted as the person's aim is to humiliate and harass me.'

She did three things. One, she blocked the harasser from her mobile; second, she deleted all her pictures from the profile so that nobody could use them again; third, she made a list of possible culprits; and fourth, took a snapshot of the messages sent by the harasser.

She shared her ordeal with her parents and later a police complaint was filed. Later, when she shared the incident with her friend Jayshree, she said, 'I am glad that you took the right actions to protect yourself from cyberbullying. It could be any one of us and I shall also remain careful in the future.' Jayshree also said that she made mistakes by posting a lot of unnecessary stuff on social media.

IN A NUTSHELL

Nothing ever goes away once it is posted online. Hence, before you post:

T: is it true?
H: is it helpful?
I: is it inspiring?
N: is it necessary?
K: is it kind?

Never share passwords or any bank-related data on dubious online sites. If you find yourself in some cyber problem, immediately inform your family, friends and the police. Always remember, the old adage 'Sticks and stones may break my bones but words will never harm me' does not apply in the cyber world, where false, hurtful and humiliating comments can go viral in just seconds and take a toll on your mental health.

11

Maintain Credible Deterrence

'It's not about being better than the other.
It's about being better than you were yesterday.'

—Jigoro Kano,
Japanese educator and judoka

According to Oxford Learner's Dictionaries, deterrent means 'Something that makes somebody less likely to do something.' Credible means something that can be believed. So, if other bullies believe that they can end up in a bad situation if they trouble you, then, your personality and attitude become a 'credible deterrent'.

A Story on Becoming a Credible Deterrent

Here is a story of a boy who learnt karate and used his skills as a credible deterrent. Once others knew he was skilled in karate, no one dared bully him.

Narender was a long-distance runner and excelled at athletics. While he pursued athletics with passion and rigour, he remained socially aloof from his peers. He was a reserved person and had few friends. In fact, some thought of him as a recluse. Seema was probably his only friend who helped him with his studies. Whenever he walked across the school corridor, he always looked at the floor. This made him a perfect target for bullies.

Amit, on the other hand, was a lively boy and was always up to fun and mischief. However, being aware that he was popular due to his lively attitude, he always looked down on his peers and jeered the introverts. 'Dude, why do you walk like a dead body and never smile?' would be Amit's usual remark at Narender. Although Narender ignored these snide remarks, he felt bad. He never confronted Amit because he felt that he was not as strong as him.

The constant feeling of being weak and worthless bothered him to the core. He hardly indulged in anything worthwhile or entertaining. One day, while flipping television channels absent-mindedly, he came across the movie, *Enter the Dragon,* starring Bruce Lee.

A few minutes into the movie, Bruce Lee had already made a strong impression on Narender with his fast moves, fighting capability and a handspring. 'Wow! What a movie! And it's just been five minutes. What a guy!' he exclaimed.

Throughout the movie, he could see Bruce Lee's character being cool-headed and as fast as lightning, taking on bad guys like O'Hara and Han. 'All of them are strong fellows,' thought Narender. None of them had a bulky physique but all of them looked fit. Bruce Lee's body radiated power, and his speed seemed unmatchable. His performance with *nunchaku*—a fighting device that has two wooden pieces tied to a chain—was extremely good.

After he finished watching the movie, Narender was charged up. On YouTube, he searched for action fights between Bruce Lee and Chuck Norris. As he watched those fights, he felt as if he was transported into a fighting ring. Narender slowly got sucked into this new world.

'These people have surely not come from Mars. If they can do it, so can I,' he thought. Inspired by Bruce Lee, he decided to learn martial arts. Though Bruce Lee had developed his own style known as *Jeet Kune Do* (the way of the intercepting fist), it was not very popular or easily available. Hence, Narender went for karate.

'If I can achieve even 10 per cent of what Lee has achieved, I would be proud of myself.' He resolved to not just learn the art of karate but also master it.

To excel at karate, he decided to learn from the best. He did some research on some of the big and well-known karate schools in his area and the style of karate taught by them. Based on his research, he came across four major styles in Karate:

- *Goju-ryu*
- *Shotokan-ryu*
- *Wado-ryu*
- *Shito-ryu*

Further, Narender found that the most popular one was the Shotokan style. Utilizing wide stances and linear techniques, this form enables students to deliver impressive strikes in a quick and efficient manner using their hands, elbows, knees and feet.

His next step was to look out for a good karate school, whose trainers could teach him Shotokan-ryu style. He finally succeeded in finding a karate school near his home that catered to his expectations. An excited Narender went to the school one day to see how it was and saw the students training under the *sensei* (teacher) who was friendly yet a strict disciplinarian.

He spoke to the instructor Shilla Grewal who in turn asked Narender to get a karate gi stitched for himself. Convinced after seeing the dojo (hall) and talking to the sensei, Narender entered the school a week later in a thick white karate gi with a white belt tied on his waist. The pants were loose so that one could stretch their legs easily. He had good stamina, but flexibility was a challenge for him. Looking into the long mirror in the locker room, he felt confident in the gi. However, he was unaware of the arduous path that lay ahead between him and his goal.

The first day was tough as Grewal took the students through the basics of karate. He beseeched each student to make serious efforts to learn the martial art of karate and never take the training casually.

A while later, the students moved on to doing 50 push-ups on their knuckles. It was painful, but according to the sensei, it was the only way to make the punches effective.

'So, boys and girls, stand in a semicircle.

'The concept of martial arts revolves around three things: motivation, discipline and time.

'Motivation must come from within to learn the craft. No one can motivate you except yourself. If you are ready to spend your parents' hard-earned money and your precious time for this craft, I would like to believe that each one of you are fully motivated to lean karate. I can teach you but it is up to you to make the best of it.

'This brings us to discipline. Unless you are disciplined, you cannot sustain the motivation for a lone time.

'The third is the time you dedicate to learn this. The more you sweat, the more you learn every day.

'Now that I have explained these basics, I take it that all of you have understood them clearly.' All students nodded in agreement.

Sensei further reminded them, 'Martial arts is not brute force. Always remember, this art must make you cool-headed and not hot-headed. This skill is for self-defence and must not be used otherwise.'

The sensei explained the grading system and the meaning of the coloured belts.

'White belt is for beginners and denotes student level 6. The next level 5 is yellow belt, level 4 is orange belt, level 3 is green belt, level 2 is blue belt and the highest level for a student, i.e., level 1 is brown belt.

Table 1

Level	Minimum Time Before Next Rank
Orange Belt	6 months of active training as an orange belt
Green Belt	9 months of active training as a green belt
Blue Belt	12 months of active training as a blue belt
Brown Belt	18 months of active training as a brown belt

Source: https://tinyurl.com/mr4dc5uf

However, the process can take more time too. The primary goal is to gain expertise and not the next level of belt.

Beyond the levels mentioned above, there are the Dan levels (black belt). It takes 4–5 years to get a black belt in karate. It can take even longer depending on your age, your natural abilities, body type, coordination levels, fitness levels, the type of sports you have done before, how much you train, how much you listen to your instructor and so on.

'Nothing is easy in life,' thought Narender, but to face bullies like Amit and redeem his pride, he was ready to sweat it out and go through the pain.

By now, the training was getting tougher by the day and Narender was kicking in with great force.

'*Whaaam*'—the sound of his kick would reverberate and he could reach out the edge of his foot up to the chin of the opponent and stop it wherever he wanted at will. This was the kind of precision required to become proficient in karate.

To boost his morale and keep himself motivated throughout the grind, he put up posters of Jet Li, Chuck Norris and Bruce Lee in his room. He used to wash his own uniform and iron it. To keep the uniform white and pristine was indeed difficult for Narender. He remembered his uncle Randhir, who was in the Indian Navy, coming to visit him in his spotlessly white uniform and wondered how his uncle managed it.

With consistent hard work, Narender managed to improve his skills. This gave a big boost to his self-esteem and once he completed his training, and later, also won a state karate championship, he went to his school principal to share this good news. The principal announced this the next day in the assembly and felicitated him in front of the entire school. He was interviewed for his school's magazine by the editorial team. He posed in front of the camera in his gi with the medal. However, as mentioned in the movie *Spider-Man*, 'With great power, comes great responsibility.' He remembered his sensei's words: 'Never use this power until and unless you are stuck in a situation where you have to use it in self-defense. Remain cool and collected and don't show off. This is an important rule of karate.'

IN A NUTSHELL

If you make yourself physically stronger and people around you know that you are not a pushover, then you will not only be able to defend yourself against any bully or any hoodlums but you will also be able to help others in distress.

12

Invest in Social Capital

'In fact, the socialization gives us the tools to fill our evolutionary roles. They are our building blocks.'

—Warren Farrell,
American political scientist

Today, in our hectic lives, it has become increasingly difficult to maintain work life balance and socialize. We have many opportunities to make new friends but many of us don't use those opportunities. For instance, one has drama clubs in the city, which provide a platform not only to display talent but also to meet new people.

A Story on the Importance of Socializing

Anil had recently joined a new school and was finding it difficult to make friends. During recess, he would be on his own and have his tiffin under a tree. The rest of the guys used to play together and enjoyed their lunch together. However, unfortunately, Anil was always left alone.

Once, he bumped into Vishal and Suraj, the two notorious bullies from his class. Since he was alone, they tried to bully him. Anil ignored their silly remarks for the first couple of days. Vishal was huge and had a bulky physique. He had a bit of hair growth on his chin, which he thought was a beard, and had a small, scanty mustache that he kept on tugging all the time while speaking.

Anil was not a loner by nature. However, he ended up being alone as he knew no one. He racked his brain to find out the best way to break the ice with his classmates.

The first thing he did was to check with his class prefect if there were any clubs or student collectives. He was told that there were plenty of clubs run by students, and all the details were available on the school website.

Anil was good with musical instruments; playing drums and other percussion instruments was his forte.

When he visited the school website, he noticed that the music club was quite active. The next day, he met Roy Mathew from Class 11, the person in charge of the music club.

Roy was a jovial fellow. When Anil met him and expressed his interest in joining the club, Roy wanted to know what instruments he played. Anil replied that he played drums. The moment Roy heard drums, he said, 'Great! We were looking for a drummer. Our drummer Sanket recently completed his schooling and is now in college. Hence, you can fill in the gap. Why don't you come in the evening? I will introduce you to our school band, The Woodies. Let me tell you, we have some good musicians.'

Anil was excited. After he was done with his classes, Roy took him to their music room. When Anil entered the music room, he was enamoured by its settings. Posters of musicians adorned the walls. There was a drum set that looked so good that his heart skipped a beat.

The room was also filled with guitars, drums, keyboards and various instruments. Soon, Roy introduced Anil to their lead guitarist Subhash, rhythm guitarist Virender, keyboard player Tanushree, lead singer Roy, and Sanjay, who played the saxophone. 'What a great combination!' thought Anil. He was keen to jump onto the bandwagon immediately. However, they wanted to see if Anil was a good drummer or not. He played a number of songs with them. Anil was pretty good at it and Roy said, 'You play well. Let us induct him in the band right away. What do you say, guys?'

The band trusted Roy's judgement. They all agreed. Tanushree said, 'We have an inter-school competition coming up in two weeks. We will get down to rehearsals from tomorrow. Anil, we practice in the evenings—6.00 p.m. to 8.30 p.m.—every day. I hope you will manage to spend this much of time for the next 15 days.'

There was no question of not being able to manage. Anil was thrilled to find a purpose. He felt as if he found a family in this group. In a blink, he made six new friends. They also introduced him to Miss Shalini Saxena, the teacher-in-charge of the group. She loved music and played Sitar during her college days.

The group got together every evening to practise for the competition. They rehearsed until the wee hours of the night and would be totally exhausted. However, they went on due to their passion for music.

On the day of the main competition, they played their best. Although they were the runners up—missing the trophy by a whisker—they were no less than winners. Anil—or Anil the drummer as he was now being referred to—struck a chord with the entire school.

The very next day, the two bullies, the burly Vishal and his sidekick Suraj, came and shook hands with him saying, 'Wow! We didn't know this hidden talent of yours. You are a gem.'

IN A NUTSHELL

Schools and colleges have different clubs and teams. It is good to join a club as it is an opportunity to socialize with others. Friends are your support system and they provide a sense of belonging.

13

An Experience to Face the World

'One's dignity may be assaulted, vandalized and cruelly mocked, but it can never be taken away unless it is surrendered.'

—Michael J. Fox,
Canadian-American actor

We all must get one thing straight: life is not a bed of roses. As human race progresses, the competition and challenges keep increasing day by day. Simplicity is a rarity, and people have become intolerant. Everyone is on a short fuse; people don't have patience and cannot tolerate any denial, leave aside insult.

In the society we live, competition starts from school, seeps into college and gets worse when you are at work. Your own colleagues will pull you down for the sake of their own progress.

In school, it is like being in a swimming pool. The water is calm and there is a lifeguard to save you if you are about to drown. There is someone to coach you on how to swim. However, once you go out of this bubble and get a job, it is like being all alone in the vast ocean—the waves are harsh and there are sharks too. Then, it is solely your responsibility to save yourself, remain afloat and swim to your destination.

Your parents and teachers can protect you—to a certain extent—when you are a child. Once you are out of school, there is no one to protect you all the time. You can't go to your boss in the office every time complaining about something or someone.

If you are planning to participate in an Ironman Triathlon, you must swim 3.8 km straight in high sea. The water is cold, the climate is harsh, and it must be done in a fixed amount of time to qualify. Where do you prepare for such a competition? You prepare in a swimming pool, covering the length of the pool 100 times daily.

Schools, therefore, become a crucible of learning life skills like a pool is to learn swimming. The more you swim in the pool, the easier it is to swim in the sea.

Schools provide you with an opportunity to learn life skills. Difficult and nasty people are a part and parcel of life. There are several people in your class with so many different talents and, therefore, you get a chance to know brilliant minds: sportsmen, swimmers, musicians, dramatists, painters. Even bullies have certain talents. However, the reason they bully people might be their own emotional and psychological problems that need to be treated with care.

Unless you learn how to fight your own battles, you will find it difficult to live a happy life in your later years. Hence, you must learn to deal with different types of kids in the school. This will eventually prepare you for life. Remember, all fingers in a hand are not the same, so deal differently with different people.

If you take this suggestion seriously, you will come out as a winner who is ready to face life. You need to get emotionally strong. Everyone is not born strong but with conscious efforts one can develop resilience. Once you decide not to give in to someone, no one can defeat you.

A Story on the Importance of Resilience

Yogi was a nice fellow, but he had a problem. He was too sweet and nice to his class fellows. Therefore, some guys used to push him around and pull his leg, and some of them were nasty enough to bully him in front of everyone. This used to happen during lunch breaks or in the school bus while returning home. He used to feel hurt but never thought of retaliating.

One day, he had been bullied badly by his classmate Harshit, who was bit of a ruffian. He had splashed ink on Yogi's shirt and Yogi had become a laughing stock. Unable to bear the humiliation, he returned home and locked himself up in his room.

His father got worried and knocked at the door: 'Yogi, please open the door. You must tell me what happened.'

After a lot of persuasion, Yogi came out, his shirt badly stained and his eyes swollen because of crying.

His dad said, 'Tell me what happened and we shall find a solution.' Yogi narrated the whole incident and told him regarding the earlier days when Harshit troubled him. His dad asked him gently, 'Why did you tolerate this for so many days?' Yogi's mother was livid upon hearing what her son had to go through.

'Please go to the school and complain to the principal,' she said. His dad replied 'I will. But before I do that, I want to speak to Yogi alone.'

He took Yogi to his room, made him sit down and gave him a glass of water. Once he saw that Yogi had calmed down, he put his hand on his shoulder and said, 'Yogi, you are now 14 years old and will go to college in another five years or so. I can come with you to the principal and complain against Harshit, and while that may stop Harshit, is there a guarantee that in future someone won't trouble you?'

Yogi looked up and said, 'Then what should I do, dad?'

His dad asked, 'How old and how big is this Harshit fellow?' Yogi said that he was of the same age and similarly built.

'Then what is the problem? You should be able to handle him yourself.'

'Tomorrow, in front of everyone, go and talk it out with him. Tell him that this is not done. He cannot throw ink on you and get away with it. Tell him that his behaviour is not appropriate and explain to him that anyone would feel bad if bullied like this. Make sure you do this in front of your friends. Try to reason it out with him. This is the first step in diplomacy.

'If he is a sensible boy he would listen and behave

himself in the future. But if he is stubborn and high headed, give him a taste of his own medicine.'

The next day, Yogi was ready to board the school bus. 'Be brave, my boy,' his dad said as Yogi walked out of the door. His mother didn't know what had been discussed between the father and the son.

As Yogi got down, he looked for Harshit. In his heart, he practised what he wanted to tell him. During the recess, he walked up to him making up his mind. He was a little scared and his heart was pounding hard. He remembered his dad's words, 'Son, be brave. It only takes one act of courage to change everything.'

Harshit was standing under a tree and was surrounded by 15 boys and girls. He was, as usual, cracking some jokes. When Yogi came to face Harshit, the latter couldn't resist the urge to chide him once again. Laughing at him, he said, 'Oh! So you are now wearing a new shirt or did your mom wash it for you?'

Yogi, as advised by his dad said, 'Harshit, please don't say such things to me. This hurts and these are bad manners in any case. How does it matter if this is a new shirt or old?'

Harshit was a hard nut to crack and had a big ego. He could not take such an answer from anyone. Shoving Yogi with his right palm, he barked, 'Yogi, I will hammer you so hard that you will not be able to come to school again!'

Yogi politely warned him again not to be rude and stop pushing him. Harshit was out of control and as he was about to punch Yogi, Yogi stopped his hand. This act of defence startled Harshit as he thought that the latter would not dare retaliate. Yogi was now a hero in front of others and above all, in front of himself.

When he reached home, he was eager to narrate the episode to his dad. His dad was happy that his son showed courage. Yogi related, 'Dad, after the incident during recess, he came to me and apologized.' His father was proud of his son. Yogi felt good about himself. Now, he was ready to face life with his head held high.

IN A NUTSHELL

Be dignified and polite in front of a bully. However, if the bully is being physical with you, you cannot take it lying down. First, you try to reason out with the person. If the person still gets physical, don't immediately resort to violent measures but make the person realize that you can retaliate if needed.

Conclusion

'The greater the force of your compassion, the greater your resilience in confronting hardships.'

—Dalai Lama

This book is a part of the attempt to teach the youth how to avoid being bullied and become independent. I hope the readers can allow this theoretical knowledge to empower themselves, become bullyproof and help others fight bullying. For this, one needs to develop the courage, assertiveness and confidence to navigate social situations and resolve their own problems. The support of peers and families is also quite helpful in handling any difficult situation one faces. Our institutions are also organized in such a way that there are systems in place to ensure one's well-being if things get out of hand. One must not be afraid to take advantage of them and report the matter to the relevant authorities as needed.

I fervently wish for every young reader to embark on a journey through childhood that is vibrant, harmonious, and free from the shadows of bullying. May this book serve as a guiding light, empowering each young soul to be confident, compassionate, and strong, to build a world where bullying has no place, and where every child can flourish without fear.

IN A NUTSHELL

For parents, here are a couple of essential tips:

Open Communication: Foster an environment of open communication at home. Encourage your children to share their experiences and concerns with you. By keeping the lines of communication open, you can better understand their challenges and provide guidance when necessary.

Teach Empathy: Instill empathy in your children by helping them understand the importance of kindness and compassion towards others. Teach them to stand up for those who may be experiencing bullying and to be an advocate for positive change.